Gallery Books
*Editor* Peter Fallon

# VENETIAN EPIGRAMS

Seán Lysaght

# VENETIAN EPIGRAMS

*Translations from Goethe*

Gallery Books

*Venetian Epigrams*
is first published
simultaneously in paperback
and in a clothbound edition
on 12 June 2008.

The Gallery Press
Loughcrew
Oldcastle
County Meath
Ireland

www.gallerypress.com

ISBN 978 1 85235 450 3  *paperback*
     978 1 85235 451 0  *clothbound*

A CIP catalogue record for this book
is available from the British Library.

# Contents

*for Martin Evans*

# Introduction

Goethe is often approached somewhat like a monument from Classical antiquity that has been obscured by time: we believe it to be of great importance but need a specialist to explain its value to us. For the English-speaking world the necessity of translation might be one aspect of this obscurity; on the other hand Dante, a figure of at least equal stature in European terms, has a vital afterlife in English translation. Some of Goethe's best translators have reinforced this difficulty: Thomas Carlyle noted 'the unwonted and in many points forbidding aspect of his chief works' while at the same time advertising Goethe's eminence; in the introduction to his own edition of the *Roman Elegies and Other Poems* Michael Hamburger referred to 'the untranslatability and elusiveness of Goethe's poetic work as a whole'.

Part of our modern difficulty with Goethe, I imagine, is that he is not like any other poet we come across. First of all the range of his interests and accomplishments seems to disperse, not reinforce, his poetic function, but this perception may be our limitation, not his. He lived at a unique time in Germany when secular learning, the reach of *Naturphilosophie*, had finally drawn clear of clerical authority; at the same time, Science had not yet become focused into academic specialisms, allowing this extraordinary man of extraordinary opportunity the chance to make an original contribution to fields as diverse as art history, architecture, geology, botany, optics and anatomy. With the scale of his energies and the diversity of his interests it is difficult for us to locate a sensibility which we could attach to our notion of what a poet should be. Even within Goethe's 'purely' literary output there are so many re-inventions, so many varieties of self-projection that it is difficult for us to relate these to a feeling individual.

Here we come up against some of the prejudices we have inherited from the Romantic movement. We are accustomed to the modern poet as someone detached from his or her society; on the other hand we find it less easy to accept that a poet might also be a botanist or a privy councillor. Introspection, reflection and recollection, a set of Wordsworthian assumptions, have more authority than we might think even in our own day. It is no accident therefore that modern figures such as Eliot, Auden and MacNeice were attentive readers and translators of Goethe. The German was a poet who could represent European culture, not just in its innocent affective origins, but in its consciously held learning as well. In his *Werther* Goethe had played the sensitive Romantic type, but he later repudiated this early success and moved towards the multi-purpose Classicism of his maturity. He was an inevitable ally for the Modernist poets who wanted poetry to be representative of its age, to engage with ideas and forms as well as the spontaneous overflow of powerful feeling.

Goethe was also modern in the care he devoted to image-management after *Werther* had made him a European celebrity. The portrait by Tischbein is just one, albeit the most famous, element in Goethe's deliberate programme of self-promotion. Against this background the *Venetian Epigrams* are especially valuable because in them Goethe gave free rein to his inclinations and only afterwards did he begin to calculate what their impact on his readers might be. Many of the impulses he has followed in the epigrams were too explicit for his milieu, and so the *Venetian Epigrams* were launched on their unsteady career of selective suppression and erasure before their eventual restoration by scholarship.

Almost one third of them were withheld from publication by Goethe and his advisors during his lifetime, and a number were destroyed by the first editors of the Weimar edition of Goethe's works. The remaining withheld epigrams were only with difficulty recovered and finally published in the early twentieth century. The present translation is the first appearance of the complete series as a separate publication in English.

For a readership accustomed to Goethe as a towering figure of literary respectability these epigrams as a whole constitute a problem. In literary terms many of them read as casual, unpolished footnotes, but even here they possess what Derek Mahon in *Adaptations* (Gallery, 2006) has called 'the idle intensity of doodles'. Thematically, they offer a unique insight into the private erotic and intellectual world of the commanding figure of Germany's Classical age. Goethe used the epigram's concise formulation to capture many essential thoughts and revealing reactions about politics, art, religion, sex and Venetian street life. Pronouncements about the recent French Revolution, for example, stand side by side with expressions of tender feeling for his young lover, Christiane Vulpius, and their new baby, as well as other responses to girls and women he encountered in Venice. Another group of epigrams, most of them suppressed during the poet's lifetime, is directed against Catholic Christianity and the iconography of the crucified Christ, which Goethe found distasteful. It is probably this last group, and not the sexually explicit epigrams, that still constitutes the most challenging element of this inheritance.

The *Venetian Epigrams* are often placed beside the earlier *Roman Elegies* in Goethe's canon and are usually as a result overshadowed by the more opulent, voluptuous poems he wrote following his return from his extended Italian sojourn in 1786-88. While the *Roman Elegies* record Goethe's exuberance at having found, at last, the classical Italy he had so long looked forward to, the *Epigrams* can seem, by contrast, tetchy and constrained. However, this is just one aspect of their surprising thematic and expressive range. The poet allowed himself such freedom in their composition that many of them had no prospect of being published in his lifetime. As Goethe's English biographer Nicholas Boyle puts it, 'Never before in his writing have views been expressed in so undramatised a form, so unattached to any *persona* other than that of Goethe at a particular time and in a particular place'. (*Goethe: The Poet and the Age*, vol. 1, pp. 660-1)

The *Venetian Epigrams* were largely written between March 31st and May 21st 1790. Goethe had travelled to Italy on this second occasion to fulfil an earlier promise to his patron Carl August, Duke of Saxe-Weimar-Eisenach, to accompany the Duke's mother, Anna Amalia, home from her Italian tour. Delays to the Duchess's trip meant that she did not reach Venice until May 6th, while social engagements and visits kept them in the city for another fortnight. The view of Goethe in Venice at this time as bored, restless, and preoccupied with Christiane and their infant son back in Weimar is only partially true. He took advantage of his time there to devote himself again to studies of Italian painting and of natural history, and to enjoy the role of *flâneur* amid the scenes of the city's varied life. The *Epigrams* also register his happiness with his situation in Weimar under Carl August's generous, indulgent patronage.

Given their controversial content, Goethe was very cautious about releasing the collection to the public. A selection of about two-thirds of the series, comprising one hundred and three epigrams, was published anonymously by Schiller in his periodical, *The Muses' Almanac*, in 1796. With a few additions, this selection remained canonical up to the 1827 edition of his works, which Goethe himself oversaw. Later in the nineteenth century, as she prepared the Weimar edition, the Grand Duchess Sophia of Saxony presided over the partial destruction of offending epigrams from the manuscripts. Most of these were subsequently recovered and published in later volumes of the Weimar edition (1910 and 1914) following the death of the Grand Duchess; a number have been irretrievably lost.

In English the *Epigrams* have had an uneven publishing history. David Luke published a generous, uninhibited selection in his Penguin edition of Goethe's *Selected Verse* in 1964. Ten years later Lewis Robert Lind published a parallel text edition of the *Roman Elegies* and *Venetian Epigrams*, including the entire series of epigrams that had been withheld during Goethe's lifetime. (While this edition cast an unsteady light on some of the obscurities of phrasing the English translations left plenty of scope for an alternative approach.) More recently a limited selection of nine epigrams was included by Michael Hamburger in his *Roman Elegies and Other Poems and Epigrams* (Anvil, 1996); a further selection of forty-one epigrams from the Venetian series appeared in David Luke and Hans Rudolf Vaget's edition of Goethe's *Erotic Poems* (Oxford World Classics, 1997).

My own translations are intended to present the *Venetian Epigrams* in their entirety as a single numbered sequence without censorship, euphemism, or the fragmentation of selection. My aim has been to deliver viable English versions that can stand without reference to the German originals. At the outset I decided to look for rhymes in English for the blank, unrhymed German. While I occasionally bent my own rule this formal requirement created a field of pressure around the translation process which called for a wider search for alternative terms and phrases. On the other hand I did not feel bound by the classical metres that Goethe occasionally used, as in the extensive tribute to his patron, Carl August. The dactylic pattern required by this metre seemed to me a stricture too far and would have inhibited the idiomatic style I was trying to keep in focus, although the six stresses of Goethe's hexameter were often a useful rule of thumb in determining the length of the line.

*Westport, 2008*

*Wie man Geld und Zeit vertan,*
*Zeigt das Büchlein lustig an.*

The little book shows, and thinks it funny,
The way you wasted time and money.

1

The heathen put lively decorations on tombs and urns:
A chorus of Bacchic women and fauns dancing about,
Making colourful rows. Creatures with cloven feet
Force a rough note free from the blaring horn.
Cymbals and drums report, the marble moves, makes music,
And you birds jostling for fruit, how gorgeous the taste in your
    beaks!
You're oblivious of all the reverberations, as is Cupid,
Whose torch lights the merry way in the motley throng.
So repletion conquers death, and the ashes within seem
To rejoice in life still, in the frozen scene.
And now I offer the richly-textured life of this page
In the hope that one day it will wrap the poet's sarcophage.


2

I had just seen the dazzling sun, the bright blue sky,
Rocky outcrops thick with wreaths of tumbling ivy,
And a winegrower tying the vine to a poplar tree —
When a balmy wind from Virgil's cradle blew towards me.
Suddenly, there were the Muses in disjointed conversation
Round their friend, the happy traveller at his destination.


3

As if she were still here, my arms hold her captive
And my heart still pushes forward to my love.
With my head still resting on her knees
I stare at those gorgeous lips, and those eyes.
Call me a wimp for how I spend my days,
I know it's no good — but wait till I tell you:
This coach has been taking me away for twenty days.

I've turned my back on the only happiness I knew.
These coachmen are unbiddable. The servants are all of a kind.
They have nothing but lies and deceit in mind,
And the only way of getting out is with the postman.
Postboys rule here — and then there's Customs!
You'll say I'm all contradictions when here I am at rest
In my lover's paradise, just like Rinaldo the blessed.
I know myself well; my body's on the move
While my soul stays back in the lap of my love.


4


This is the Italy I left, the roads still dusting over,
The visitor fleeced even if he keeps looking over his shoulder.
You search in vain for German honesty in every corner:
Everything's hustle and bustle, but no good breeding and no order
They're all out for what they can get, they're suspicious and vain,
And it's the same story among the nobility at court.
A beautiful country! But I'll never find Faustina again.
This isn't the same Italy I left with a heavy heart.


5


I lay stretched in the gondola and steered among the boats
That float in the Grand Canal, many of them laden down.
You'll find all kinds of produce there for every taste,
Wheat, vegetables, every kind of timber, wine.
As the gondola bolted through a stray laurel berry
Stung my cheek. I shouted, 'Daphne, are you out to get me?
Don't I deserve better!' The nymph whispered then — and smiled
'Be quiet! The penalty's light. A poet's crimes are mild.'

### 6

Whenever I see a pilgrim I'm overcome by emotion.
The way human beings are inspired by false notions!

### 7

Nazarene! You saved your people well with suffering
And miracles — but what option have your followers now?
As Christians, they are meant to live and bring up children,
But all that vital joy means nothing to your dismal power.
A sound young man who sets his heart against corruption
Will find himself tormented by his own desires.
Come down again and suffer, you God of creation,
Come and save your people from their compounded pain,
Cut off the source of joy and life by working wonders
And, Stephen, I'll play the part of Paul, as you require.

### 8

I had a sweetheart once, the dearest thing I had!
But now she's gone from me! You'll get over it. Enough said.

### 9

The gondola is like a cradle, the way it gently rocks,
And just like a roomy coffin is the projecting box.
Proper order! We all wobble and drift between the cradle and
    the grave
Without a care on the Grand Canal to the end of our days.

## 10

There goes the Nuncio beside the Doge in stately procession
To the burial of a lord. One of them seals the grave.
I don't know what the Doge thinks of this, but the other one
Smiles at the solemnity of the great charade.

## 11

What's the rush? Why all the shouting? People need to eat,
To raise children and feed them as best they can.
Take note, traveller, and do the same at home.
To do that well is enough for any man.

## 12

When a master chef prepares a rich banquet for his guests
He makes his food a blend of different ingredients.
You enjoy this little book in the same way, and can hardly tell
The different things you like. No matter, here's to your health.

## 13

Who shall I give this book to? To the Duchess who gave it to me.
She is the one who provided an Italy in Germany.

## 14

'You have the nerve to write unseemly things in German?' —
    My friend,
It may be German to us but it's Greek to the rest of the world.

15

Naugerius burnt Martial because his taste was too fastidious.
Will you throw away the silver because it isn't gold, you idiot?


16

Horace earned the little he desired. You can wish for less
With greater merit and still lack his success.


17

Would you listen to those clerics! How they've made it their
     business
To turn up and just spout, day in, day out.
I won't have a word said against them; they've understood this:
He's a happy fellow who's still blethering on tomorrow!


18

St Mark's on Holy Thursday evening, a conman priest
Appears on stage to show us remnants of his god,
When a crazy girl in blind, hysterical frenzy cries,
'Show us the relics! Show us the relics of the Lord!'
Ah, what use to you is a piece of him who slackened on the cross?
What you need is a little part of that fellow from Lampsacus.


19

Our Lord liked to live among sinners and women on the game.
This doesn't surprise me; you know, with me it's the same.

### 20

'Why would you be so cruel as to take away from a Christian
The serenity of his belief?' Not me, no one can.
Doesn't the Bible say, 'The heathens can argue all they please.'
You see, I'm proof of Scripture, so read it, and depend on me.


### 21

Fanatics gather followers like sand by the sea.
Sand is sand. O my wise friend, be the pearl for me.


### 22

It's wonderful, in spring, to go barefoot on budding clover,
And run a gentle hand along the lamb's fleece.
It's wonderful to see revived branches covered all over
With blossom, and the lush new growth attracting notice,
But even better to make love to a country girl in celebration.
Failing this, May has many pleasures to offer in compensation.


### 23

Here the ruler is like a hammer, the country an anvil,
And the people hunched up like tin in the middle.
Ah, the poor tin, when random blows
Are ineffective, and the finished kettle never shows!


### 24

While the wise man's friends are few in number
The fanatic wins plenty of followers and stirs the crowd.

Pictures of heroic scenes are usually mediocre,
Works of genius and skill not for the multitude.


25

How they all love a botcher! I'm almost taken in
By the myth that says I'm a botched creation.


26

Vulgarity attracts them all. You can be sure,
When you see lots of people doing something fast, it's vulgar.


27

The guy we voted in is going to cream it.
He told us we would win — or did we dream it?


28

'If only we could open the eyes of the world!' — That'll be the day!
Better to mind your own business and find your own way.


29

On a hero's path to glory thousands pay the price.
Don't blame the poet if he takes a conqueror's advice.

## 30

They say poverty leads to God. If you're in any doubt,
Go to Italy as a tourist. You'll soon find out.

## 31

If you want someone to give out to make sure it's not a saint,
Because an upright man forgives and always shows restraint.

## 32

Crabs with naked arses, in search of an empty shell
To crawl into and imagine this is a house of their own
Are funny creatures — they're hungry, but they're cute as well.
I had this thought when I saw them on the seashore.
How right Lavater was when he said, 'Christian and Man are the
   same.'
Correct! The Christians use human reason to cover their naked
   shame.

## 33

When I was a kid I was mad about a puppet show.
For a long time it kept me enthralled, until I smashed it.
Similarly, Lavater reached for the crucified doll when he was small:
He can cuddle it until he breathes his last, the fool!

## 34

He writes, addressing the good, well, he can pull the other one.
They must be good to read this nonsense and believe it.

Then he writes addressing the wise. I'll never know them.
If that's wisdom, by God, I'm glad to be an idiot.


35

Look at the crush of bodies around that shop! And look how fast
They weigh it, get the money, and hand out the stuff!
There's a rush on hellebore, to save people going to the doctor;
So instead of proper medication, they're selling snuff.


36

Any nobleman in Venice can become the Doge,
So even as boys they're refined, special, measured, and proud.
No wonder the wafers are so tender in the Catholic south
When the priest consecrates God from the same dough.


37

Two ancient Greek lions stand calmly at the Arsenal.
The pair dwarf the city gates, the towers and canals.
If the mother of the gods appeared both of them
Would fawn at her chariot, and she'd be pleased with her team.
But now they look sad; a tomcat newly decked with wings
Purrs everywhere because Venice has adopted him.


38

The pilgrim sets out briskly! And will he find the saint,
Will he hear and see the man who worked the miracle?

No, time has taken him away, you only find remains,
His skull, and a few of his bones kept as relics.
We're all pilgrims, looking for Italy, we're all at the same thing,
Rejoicing at lost fragments of bone and worshipping.


### 39

Jupiter Pluvius, today you come to us a friendly demon;
You give us a multiple gift in the one moment,
You slake the city's thirst and give new growth to the land,
And in my little book you foster more epigrams.


### 40

Pour away! Flood the dusty land — let it bring forth broccoli!
Give those frogs in their redcoats all the water they want.
Just don't penetrate my little book; to me
It's a flask of pure elixir, not anyone's bowl of punch.


### 41

That's the church of St John-in-the-Muck — too right!
My new name for Venice is St Mark-in-the-Shite.


### 42

You poor unfortunate frogs, Venice is all you've known!
If you jump out of the water you land on hard stone.

## 43

If you've been to Baia you know the sea and fishes.
This is Venice now, so you know the frogs and ditches.


## 44

'Are you still asleep!' Be quiet, let me rest. When I wake
I think, What am I doing here? The bed is wide, but bleak.
I think I'm in Sardinia, where everyone sleeps alone,
When it's Tivoli I need, where you're woken by your loved one.


## 45

All nine of them used to come, I mean the Muses.
Not that it mattered to me, if a girl was on my lap.
Then I left my darling, I was abandoned by those daughters.
Things got so desperate I was tempted by the rope.
But heaven is a crowded place and the gods have their uses.
At last I hailed thee, Boredom, mother of the Muses!


## 46

You ask me what kind of girl I want? But I have her,
Just the one I want, I mean, so much in one small part.
I went down to the sea and looked for mussels. I discovered
A little pearl in one and now I keep it by my heart.


## 47

All the things I've attempted! Drawing, copper etching,
Oil painting, I've even tried my hand at modelling clay —

But only occasionally, with no skill, and no tangible gain.
The only gift I brought to perfection in any way
Is writing German, and so, poor poet that I am,
I waste my life and art in this wretched medium.


### 48

You beg with covered faces and pretty children in your arms
And so you make a powerful plea to the manly heart.
Everyone wants a little boy to match your urchin's charms
And every man imagines the veil disguises a sweetheart.


### 49

All women are commodities; they vary in price
Whenever a hard-up fellow decides he has to do business.
A respectable girl is lucky if she finds her gentleman.
She sells herself just once, and then the deal is done.


### 50

'Did Hymen escape you? Or did you avoid him?' — What can I
    say about
Hymen? He's a comfort, but he's too serious for me.
You shouldn't blab about the marriage bed, and poets are blab-
    mouths,
But free love gives our tongues the courage to be free.

## 51

I called the little girl, 'Little girl, is your master not at home?'
But she would not answer. She was not a little girl any more.


## 52

In the narrowest of streets — barely room to get through —
A girl sat in my way as I was exploring the town.
She was as gorgeous as the place, and I was seduced.
Gosh, the tourist found another passageway open!
If you had a girl for every canal, Venice, and pussy
Like your little streets, you'd be a magnificent city.


## 53

That's not your child you're begging with, to win me over.
If you really want to move me, bring me my own lover!


## 54

When I meet you today you lick your lips and keep walking.
Is your tongue trying to tell me you never stop talking?


## 55

The Germans study and practise all of the arts; they have
A wonderful aptitude for anything they take on properly.
There's just one art they practise and will not study: poetry.
And, as we know, my friends, this one they do sloppily.

## 56

You gods, you've often said you're on the poet's side
So give him his whole range of modest needs.
Proper lodgings first of all, then plain food and drink.
The Germans, like you, are fond of the nectar.
Then decent clothes, and friends for private banter,
And a bedfellow in the evening who loves him with her heart.
These five normal things are my basic demands,
And then I ask for languages, ancient and modern,
To learn the ways of people and their past.
Give me sensibility, as you have shown it in the arts,
And then a popular reputation, helped along by those in power –
And whatever else people think being famous can confer.
Good. And now my thanks to you gods, the happiest of men
Is in the making, since most of these you've already given.

## 57

Of course my duke isn't the biggest of Germany's princes,
He doesn't have a lot of power, his territory isn't extensive.
But if every prince used his influence
At home and abroad as he does, you would raise a glass to the
    Germans.
But why sing his praise when his work is there for all to see?
Are you getting paid to compose all this flattery?
No, but he gave me things you would not expect from a prince:
A house with garden and grounds, free time, support and trust.
I had no one to thank but him for seeing to all my needs.
As a poet I had no talent for making ends meet.
If I was big in Europe, what did Europe ever give me?
Nothing! I paid for my own poems and paid for them dearly.
I had many German imitators and many French readers
And, England, you've kindly taken in this bedraggled caller.
But what use is it to me if the overworked Chinese

Are painting Werther and Lotte on their souvenirs?
No king went to any trouble. No emperor bothered to ask
How I got on — but he was my Caesar and Maecenas.


58

What does a life amount to? Thousands can discuss
A man's achievements and how he got things done.
Thousands more can enjoy a little verse
While thousands demur. Just live my friend, sing on!


59

I'd become totally weary from viewing all those pictures,
Those splendid treasures of art that Venice has in its keep.
Even that pursuit takes time, you have to get some sleep,
And then, my exhausted eyes needed live entertainment.
You trickster! I saw that you were the model of those boys
In Giovanni Bellini, painted with the wings of angels,
Bearing cups to the bridegroom in Paolo Veronese
Where the wedding guests drank water, and believed in miracles.


60

I could just make out the cage where a lovely choir of girls
Sang in their busy, bustling life behind a grille.
Girls usually wear us out. But Venice, fair dues,
We are well entertained by the girls you produce.

## 61

This sweet little figure shaped as if by an artist's hand,
Supple, and apparently boneless, like an invertebrate swimming
    along.
So many limbs and joints for everyone's pleasure,
And beautifully responsive, made to perfect measure.
I've known lots of different people, all kinds of fish and fowl,
And the strangest creepy-crawlies from nature's manifold,
And still you amaze me, Bettina, you sweet little wonder,
You're all of these together, and an angel, what's more.


## 62

Careful how you turn your feet skywards, you sweet little thing.
Jupiter, the rogue, will see you; you'll have Ganymede worrying.


## 63

My biggest worry is this: Bettina is developing her skills,
Every one of her little limbs is getting more supple.
One day she'll put her tongue into her dainty little twat.
Be able to bring herself off. She won't need a man for that.


## 64

When you spread your lovely thighs at your father's signal
Your private place sinks down to touch the floor. Little girl,
One day your first lover will find your flower has gone.
That part was lost to your livelihood early on.

65

Stretch your toes to heaven, with a mind that's free of care.
We're not innocent like you when we raise our arms in prayer.


66

No wonder your little neck leans to one side. It has to carry
Your whole body. You may be light, but too much for your throat.
I don't mind it at all, that steep posture of your head;
No neck ever bent under a prettier load.


67

Just as Bruegel bewilders our roving eye with his monstrous images
As they merge and interweave in their hellish blur,
And Dürer blows our minds as well with his scenes
From the Apocalypse, with men and monsters,
And with the power of words in our enraptured ears
A poet stirs our curiosity with his sphinxes, sirens and centaurs,
And in this way, in troubled dreams, you think you grip
On steady things and make progress forward — when everything
    slips.
So does Bettina dazzle us with her skills as an athlete
And also delights when she lands on the soles of her feet.


68

I would gladly cross that line Bettina draws in chalk.
The child sets out her stall to push me gently back.

### 69

'Would you look at those souls! Is God here at all?
They're a pile of dirty clothes you'd carry to the well.
Oh! She'll fall! I can't bear to look! Let's go! So graceful!
The way she stands, so light; you can see she's enjoying it.'
Old lady, you're right to admire Bettina. In your delight you seem
Younger and more beautiful, like my little queen.

### 70

I like everything about you. What gives me the greatest thrill
Is when your father's two hands toss you up over yourself.
You flip yourself over and then, after dicing with death,
You land on your feet and walk again, scarcely out of breath.

### 71

Every face relaxes at once; all the furrows are gone
That marked fatigue, poverty and worry; happiness looks on.
The heart of the sailor melts and he taps you on the face.
He may be stingy but he still gets out his purse,
And the citizens of Venice contribute as they open their cloaks
As if you'd begged in the name of St Anthony's works,
And Our Lord's five wounds, and the heart of the Virgin, Most
    Blessed,
And in the name of the holy terror that makes us fear God.
Every sailor, vendor and beggarman joins every little boy
To press forward with excitement. You make them children in
    their joy.

72

You've raised four lovely children to be performers,
You old trickster, and now you send them round, cap in hand.
'I keep my possessions about me,' the wise one said.
'My possessions,' says you, 'are ones I've made myself.'


73

You old fantasist, you call your little girl an American.
Didn't you make her here in Europe, you lucky man?


74

'Best wishes to you all. You're very kind!' you say as you hold out
The little plate and thank me in your gorgeous way.
Ah, you're already my best wish, and if only you were older
We could be two of a kind until the break of day.


75

Ladies, if we fancy the girl, you shouldn't disapprove.
She gets us aroused in the evening to serve your night of love.


76

The craft of poetry is amusing, but it comes at a cost.
As the little book gets fatter, think of all the money lost.

77

'Why can't you move on? What has come over you, you waster?
You're writing reams about this girl. Begin something smarter.'
Give me a chance. I'll sing in good time about leaders and kings
Once I've mastered the plot of their comings and goings.
In the meantime I'll sing of Bettina because we're very close kin,
We poets and jugglers, we're always glad to meet up again.


78

'Goats to the left!' The judge will direct one day.
'And you little sheep, stand quietly to my right,' he'll say.
Good! But let's hope he says one more thing:
'Now put the sensible people where I can see them!'


79

To keep me churning out these epigrams you must
Keep me away from my sweetheart at all costs!


80

I never liked those radicals preaching freedom.
It's their own greed for power that drives each of them.
To set people free, be generous to those you know.
And to see how dangerous that is, have a go!


81

Kings and demagogues are the same, they want the best —
Or so it's said, mistakenly: they're only human, like us.

The masses can never agree on the common good, we know it:
If there's anyone who feels a general desire let him show it.


82

Once they get to thirty I want every radical nailed to a cross.
As soon as a fool gets sense he's on a mission, and dangerous.


83

A trinity has you conned, of priest, politician and teacher,
And you people pray to this shamrock from the bottom of your
    heart.
Now there's hardly a clear thought or word anywhere
Without grave offence to God, morality, or the state.


84

Puffed-up Christian pride prefers the miracles of the Lord
To the despised feats of heroes and the teachings of sages,
And yet it's happy to wear the spoils the pagan left behind
As the borrowed style for itself and its naked saviour,
Just as precious candlelight is gathered by the priest
Around his God, the branded, consecrated host.


85

Many followed you blindly and went off the rails
Of this ordinary life, the way it also happened to you.
I can't follow. I want to reach the end of my days

As a sensible man, and I want to be satisfied too.
Still, today I follow you as I choose the mountain path
And this time I see you've lost your tongue, King of the Jews.


86

'The grave is open! It's a great miracle! The Lord is risen!'
Or so they think! You rogues, you've made off with him.


87

Stoics and Christians, they all teach the same thing:
For a free man Stoic or Christian is not an option.


88

A saintly Christian radical says, 'Jews and Christians out!'
Then it's Christians and heathens in a bearded Jewish curse.
'Put the Christians to the sword and set the Jews alight.'
A Turkish child sings this, to mock them both.
Which of them is right? You've got to decide.
If these are the fools God keeps in house I'll pass by.


89

You're more like ghosts from hell than Christians, you Screamers.
I'm wide awake. The chance of delicious sleep is gone.
Why does the priest perform so many thousands of gestures
And not banish you all back to hell again?

## 90

If the upper classes resent France's unhappy fate,
Then the lower classes should lament it even more.
Who would protect the crowd from itself when the great
Were ruined, when the crowd was in the crowd's power?

## 91

I have lived through crazy times, and I also conspired
To be crazy myself, as the time required.

## 92

'Hey, isn't this how it's done? We have to dupe the common herd.
Just look at them, they're so gormless and so ill-bred.'
That's how everyone is at the start of their education.
But let's be decent now and teach them some civilization.

## 93

Princes often stamp their faces on copper with thin silver plate
And so, for a long time, the people let themselves be fooled.
Fanatics put the mark of truth on nonsense and deceit,
And for want of a touchstone people think this is genuine gold.

## 94

You say those guys are crazy, meaning that loud rant
We hear in the streets and market squares of France.
I think they're crazy too. You have one guy raving
About home truths, while wisdom is silent in others slaving.

## 95

Traditionally the nobility spoke *français*,
And anyone who wasn't fluent was scarcely heard.
Now everyone is delighted to speak this way
So, nobles, don't object: What you wanted has occurred.

## 96

'Epigrams, don't be so bold!' Why not? We are headings only.
The real world has the chapters of the story.

## 97

As God gave a bag of meat to Peter, putting every animal in,
Take this little book, my friends, showing virtue and sin.

## 98

Whether an epigram is any good is hard to know.
You can't keep track of your own thoughts, you rogue.

## 99

I'm sure it gets easier to understand this little verse
The cruder it is, the more malicious and more envious.

## 100

Chloe swears she loves me; I don't think so. 'But she does!'
Fine, but if I listened to the experts it would be the end of us.

## 101

You love no one, Philarchos, yet you love me with such duress.
Have you no other way of conquering me than this?

## 102

The meaning of God, Man, the Universe — is it really such a
  secret?
No! It's only a secret because no one wants to hear it.

## 103

I'm like a saint, the way I put up with lots of things.
I can suffer most irritations with stoic patience.
A few things I can't cope with, although I've tried:
Tobacco smoke, bed bugs, garlic, and Christ crucified.

## 104

For a long time I've wanted to tell you about those little beasts
That move back and forth so gracefully and so fast.
They're just like little snakes, with four legs; they run,
Creep and scuttle, and drag their little tails away at last.
Look at them there — and there! And now they've disappeared!
I wonder what crevice or what bush has taken them in.
As I'm going to use them as a pleasant device,
From now on, with your permission, I'll call them *lacerten*.

## 105

If you've seen *lacerten* you can imagine those girls
As they move about in their finery all over the square.
They're so fast and agile as they glide and stop to gossip
And their costumes rustle softly behind them. There!
There's one. And there! Once you've lost her, there's no point
In going after her; she won't show herself again so soon.
But if you don't mind corners, alleyways and stairs,
Follow her right into her *spelunca* when she gives you the come-on


## 106

I suppose you want to know what a *spelunca* is? (You see
This book of epigrams is nearly becoming a dictionary.)
It means gloomy houses in narrow little streets
Where you follow a beautiful woman's invitation for coffee
And she's the one who looks busy, not you.


## 107

When she says, 'Let's go for coffee, stranger,' she wants to
    masturbate me.
Wasn't I right all along, my friends, to hate coffee?


## 108

Two of the finest *lacerten* are always side by side.
One is that bit short, the other that bit tall.
If you have to choose between them it's impossible to decide.
You'd say either, on her own, was the prettiest of all.

## 109

'You're not from here, sir, are you? Are you from Venice?'
Said these two *lacerten* when they got me into their house.
Guess! — You're a Frenchman! A Neapolitan!
And so, as they drank their coffee, they chattered on.
Then the pretty one said, 'Now, let's get started,' and put down
    her cup.
Straight away I could feel her hand trying to work me up.
I grabbed it gently and held it tight. Then the other one wanted
    to do
The same with her dainty little finger, and I had to fend her
    off too.
'Ah! He's a foreigner!' said the two of them. They had a laugh then,
And they pestered me for gifts and got a few, reluctantly given,
And they pointed out another apartment farther on
For the later hours of night, and hotter fun.
If these creatures knew the stranger straight away by his refusal,
    surely
You can tell why the men of Venice look so poorly.


## 110

They say that saints have a special wish for sinners,
To save them from hell. That's just how I feel as well.


## 111

'If I were a settled wife and had all my wants supplied
I'd be full of cheer and true, I would hug and kiss my man.'
These were the words she sang, that little whore in Venice,
The purest prayer you heard, in all her bawdy songs.

## 112

A dog is a man's best friend — what's so amazing about this?
They both go for the rear end. Both stop in the street for a piss.


## 113

Give me another word for it, instead of 'Schwanz', O Priapus,
Because this is my predicament as a poet in German.
I'd call you Phallus in Greek, and that would sound pompous.
'Mentula' is the Latin word, from *mens* or mind.
The Schwanz is the tail, it comes from behind,
And that was never my kind of thing, from behind.


## 114

Camper Junior held forth in Rome on his father's
Analysis of animals: how they were created by nature,
Given organs such as stomachs, then necks, paws and tails,
All this in halting German and ideas that were not his.
At the end he said, 'Now there we have it, the beast on four
    feet.
And now, my friends, copulation is all we need.'
Poor Camper, you paid a heavy price for that slip of the tongue.
After that you had to swallow mercury eight days long.


## 115

I liked boys as well, but I prefer girls;
If I've had enough of them as girls they'll still do as boys.

## 116

I own expensive rings! Engraved, sumptuous stones
Of superior design and style set in pure gold.
They're expensive, these dazzling gems,
You've seen them glitter at the table where we play games.
But there's another little ring I know from another source,
The one old Hans Carvel used to own when he was old.
He shouldn't have stuck his smallest finger into that ring,
Only his biggest finger, the eleventh, belonged therein.


## 117

I know I'm getting cocky; that's no surprise. You gods will vouch,
And you're not the only ones, I'm also loyal and devout.


## 118

'Did you not meet polite society? Your little book of verse
Has no one but jugglers and ruffians, and even worse.'
I did meet polite society. 'Polite' is when
You couldn't write the tiniest little poem about any of them.


## 119

That's a brave question, to wonder what Destiny meant
By me? In many cases, usually not a lot.
A poet might have been her great achievement
If only words hadn't been such a stumbling block.

120

'You devote yourself to botany? To optics? What are you at?
Wouldn't you be better off to get involved with a tender heart?'
No. What keeps me going is my involvement with nature.
As for affairs of the heart, sure any gobshite can do that!


121

Newton put all the colours together to make pure white. Then he
Used this whitewash to dazzle you for a century.


122

A student says to me, 'They really make sense to us,
These theories we get from the professor. He's so wise.'
Once you have the right design for a timber cross
You can easily lay out a living body to be crucified.


123

If a young lad misses his girl on a difficult journey
He can read this little book to take his mind off it.
And if some day a girl is waiting for her lover she can
Have this little book till he comes — and then get rid of it.


124

Like the gesture of the girl who fondly stroked
My arm in secret as she hurried past,
O Muses!, allow this traveller the favour of short poems,
And keep your friend's greatest privileges till last.

## 125

When the sun sends cloudy, misty days that are overcast
How subdued we are as we walk along the paths!
And when it's lashing rain on the traveller what a welcome relief
On a stormy night is the cosy shelter of a country roof.
But quick, clear those clouds out of your face!
She's on her way back! Be like the Nature goddess!


## 126

If the pure feeling of love's pleasures is what you're after
Remember that Cupid is neither solemn nor obscene.
If you're too serious you'll spoil his easy laughter;
Too gross, and the cheeky imp deserts the scene.


## 127

God of the Poppy, Morpheus, you can't tempt me with your drug.
I prefer to stay alert. The thing I want is love.


## 128

You fill me with love, and with desire; I feel it, I'm on fire.
Now, my love, it's some trust you need to inspire.


## 129

Eros, I know you as well as the next man. Hey!
It's your torch in the dark that lights us on our way.
But then you lead us into strange paths we cannot distinguish
Where we really need your beam, and the poor light is extinguished.

## 130

You say be patient — with just one night at your heart!
With boss Cupid in the dark keeping us apart!
And now, it's the morning, when Aurora listens in
On the lovers breast to breast, and early Phoebus wakes them.

## 131

'If you mean it stop hesitating and give me a kiss.'
You must be joking. Sweetheart, I've had enough of this.

## 132

What can I say? You're annoyed because I don't speak.
With all those sighs you're missing the meaning of my look.
There's only one goddess who can break the seal of my lips,
Only Aurora, who woke me one time beside you as I slept.
Then, to greet the gods of morning, I can sing my hymn
Like the fondly chanted secrets of the figure Memnon.

## 133

That's a funny trick! No sooner is the disc released
Than it spins up to the hand again, on a skein.
You know, this is how I thought I threw my heart
At a series of women, but it always flew back again.

## 134

Oh, I used to follow all the seasons of the turning year.
I'd look forward to Lent, and I couldn't wait for the fall of leaves.

But now with Cupid's pinions whirring in my ear
It's always spring, and I've abandoned nature studies.


135

You ask me how I live, I'll tell you: I'm alive.
If I had a thousand years I wouldn't want it otherwise.


136

Ye gods, how should I thank you for all you've given me, everything
I ever asked for? — which usually meant next to nothing!


137

To climb the highest peak in the morning twilight
And greet the day's herald, O you welcoming star!
What a thrill as a young man, enticed out at night
Repeatedly, to wait nervously for the sky-queen to appear!
Now my dearest love makes the new day arise
And the sun always comes too soon in her heavenly eyes.


138

You're all amazed and point to the sea tonight: it seems on fire,
The way the waves move in flames around the ship!
That's not surprising if you think of it; the sea bore Venus,
And wasn't Cupid, her son, the god of burning passion?

## 139

I saw the sparkling sea and the twinkling waves,
With a brisk wind in their favour the sails moved on —
I was all indifferent to this. My dream-dimmed eyes
Longed for the memory of those snowy mountains.
The south has many fine things, but what attracts
Is someone in the north, irresistibly drawing me back.


## 140

Everyone tells me, child, that you're making a fool of me.
Just carry on. I'll be made a fool of willingly.


## 141

What do I live for, you ask? Just this, it keeps my heart engaged:
To be with my love tomorrow, whom I haven't seen for eight days.


## 142

My friends, all of your challenges I'll meet head on.
But sadly I just can't manage to sleep alone.


## 143

You won't lie naked beside me, you gorgeous thing,
You keep yourself wrapped up modestly in the covers.
Tell me, is it your body or your dress I'm desiring?
Modesty is a dress that doesn't belong between lovers.

144

For a long time, in search of a soul-mate, the most I got was a ride,
But when I made a pass at you, you little slut, I found a bride.


145

When I first tried love, every time I was spurned.
Whatever about that sport it can't beat love returned.


146

Dear girl, don't be afraid of the snake before you on the path.
Just ask the priest. That's the one Eve was friendly with.


147

My friends, I couldn't say for sure if all that Moses
And the prophets said was fulfilled in the risen Christ.
But one thing I do know: the dreams, desires and wishes
That come true when my sweet love is sleeping on my breast.


148

The world is wide and beautiful, but I am grateful to heaven
That there's a narrow little garden I can call my own.
Take me back home. A gardener has no business being away!
He's only happy and fulfilled if he tends it every day.

## 149

Ah, her head is sinking, the lovely rosebud! Who
Will quickly pour refreshing water on her roots?
So she's happy to come into leaf, and the time she spends
In flower lasts for a while, and the fruit ripens in the end.
But my head wilts as well with worry and fatigue.
Dear girl! A glass of sparkling wine is what I need.


## 150

Oh! My girl is leaving! She's embarking! — My king
Aeolus, mighty Lord!, hold back the storms!
'You fool!' the god calls out. 'It's not storms you have to worry
    about:
It's the little wind, when gentle Cupid flaps his wings!'


## 151

She was poor, when I met her, without a dress to her name.
In those days I liked her naked; today it's the same.


## 152

I often lost the run of myself, and then came to my senses,
But this girl gives me the greatest happiness I've known.
If this is another mistake, ye gods, protect me,
Just spare me the sober truth until I get home.

### 153

Yours was a sad gift, Midas: in your trembling hands
You felt heavy, transmuted treasure, you hungry old man.
My lot is happier, although it's a similar case;
I change things instantly into luminous verse.
Noble Muses, I don't complain; just don't change
My love, when I press her to my breast, into a fairy tale.


### 154

'Ah, my throat is a bit swollen,' she said anxiously.
There now, my child, be quiet and listen to me.
You've been touched by the hand of Aphrodite. This is a sign
Of irreversible change for your little body.
She'll soon spoil your slim figure and neat little breasts.
Everything's going to fatten; none of your new clothes will fit.
But don't worry. A fading flower is a sign for the nurseryman
That the lovely, increasing fruit will come good in autumn.


### 155

It's delightful to hold your sweetheart in your arms
When her beating heart confesses love for the first time.
Even better to feel the kicking of the little one
As it develops, moving in the cherished womb.
The child is practising the moves of senseless youth already;
It knocks to ask for the light of day so soon.
Patience for a few more days! You'll find that Destiny
Requires a strict lead from the seasons on all life's avenues.
Whatever may happen to you, you lovely growing baby —
May you be granted love, because love made thee!

156

Naively, I used to think I could learn something from others.
I was forty years of age before I realized I was wrong.
To think that others could teach me has always been my error;
According to each one's need, let his Fate teach every man.


157

O holy Sun, I've always paid you a joyful tribute
Whenever you appeared from thick clouds or mist,
But when you emerged after rain, and steam rose from the gondol:
Never as happily as in the slough of Venice.


158

And so I spent my time in the city of Poseidon
Deprived of any pleasure, whole days gone down the drain,
But I had sweet dreams and sweet memories to savour.
Without these two, what life has any flavour?

# Notes

3 *Rinaldo the blessed*, hero of Torquato Tasso's poem, *Jerusalem Delivered*. Tasso was the subject of a major play completed by Goethe in 1789.

4 *Faustina*, the Roman woman with whom Goethe is reputed to have had his first sexual experience, in 1788, when he was thirty-eight.

15 *Naugerius*. To express his contempt of their content, the Venetian Andreas Naugerius (1483-1529) is said to have held a ritual burning of the works of Martial every year.

18 *Lampsacus*, a locality on the Hellespont where the cult of Priapus supposedly originated. Priapus is a god of sexual potency, often represented as an ithyphallic figure; he is invoked in the *Roman Elegies* and *Venetian Epigrams* to celebrate Goethe's recent sexual fulfilment.

32 *Lavater*. Johann Caspar Lavater, Swiss pastor and theologian with whom Goethe had a long-running and increasingly acrimonious debate about Christianity.

35 *Hellebore*, an ingredient in snuff.

41 *St John-in-the-Muck*, a reference to the church of San Giovanni in Bragora, which in turn refers to muddy lowlands near the original site.

43 *Baia*, an ancient Roman resort in the Bay of Pozzuoli, north of Naples.

57 *Maecenas*, an influential literary patron in Augustan Rome, especially of Virgil. Here Goethe pays tribute to his patron, Duke Carl August of Saxe-Weimar-Eisenach. Goethe went to Weimar at the Duke's invitation in 1775, at the age of twenty-six, and was based there for the rest of his life.

59 *You trickster*. Bettina, a young girl performer of great agility. This is the first in a series of epigrams about a troupe of street entertainers in Venice.

60 *the cage where a lovely choir of girls/Sang*. One of the attractions in Venice at this time was the female choir at the church of San Lazzaro dei Mendicanti, where the singers remained hidden from the congregation.

62 *Ganymede*, a boy of great beauty, cupbearer to Jupiter.

101 *Philarchos*, derived from Greek, meaning 'power hungry'.

113 *Schwanz*, 'tail', also meaning 'penis' colloquially.

114 *Camper Junior*. Adrian Gilles Camper (1759-1820), son of the Dutch anatomist Petrus Camper, who had earlier rejected Goethe's published findings about the existence of an inter-maxillary bone in the human skull. Camper gave lectures in Rome on his father's work until he fell ill with syphilis, for which the cure in those days was doses of mercury.

116 *Hans Carvel*, a rich old jeweller in Jean de Lafontaine's story 'Hans Carvel's Ring'. The ring is given to the central figure to guarantee his young wife's faithfulness.

121 *Newton*. The science of optics and Newton's theory of colour were among Goethe's main scientific preoccupations at this time. He insisted on publishing this epigram in the *Muses' Almanac* selection of 1796, despite the reluctance of his friend Schiller.

137 *To climb the highest peak in the morning twilight.* Goethe is here describing one of the favourite excursions of the early Alpinists and Romantics. Wordsworth's account of a similar nocturnal outing on Snowdon is given in the *Prelude*, Book XIII. The Irish scientists Sir William Wilde and Robert Lloyd Praeger reported on similar experiences on Tenerife in 1837 and 1927 respectively.

151 *She was poor, when I met her.* This is the first in a series of epigrams about Christiane Vulpius, the young woman whom Goethe met shortly after his return from the main Italian trip. Their subsequent *union libre*, with Christiane established as mistress of his house in the Ilm Park, caused some scandal in the court society at Weimar and alienated Goethe's earlier confidante Charlotte von Stein. Undeterred, Goethe celebrated their relationship in the *Roman Elegies*. Their son August was born at Christmas in 1790, three months before Goethe's return to Italy.

# Acknowledgements

I am indebted to David Luke's pioneering edition of Goethe's *Selected Verse*, originally published by Penguin in 1964 and several times revised. Lewis Robert Lind's parallel text edition of the *Roman Elegies and Venetian Epigrams* (Kansas UP, 1974) resolved a few of my difficulties with the original German while at the same time encouraging my search for a fresher idiomatic translation. Several local and topical references in the epigrams were explained by the notes in Jochen Golz and Rosalinde Gothe's facsimile edition of the manuscripts, *Goethe: Venezianische Epigramme* (Insel Verlag, 1999). Any English-language reader interested in Goethe will be drawn to Nicholas Boyle's extraordinary account of his life and times, *Goethe: The Poet and the Age* (Oxford, 1991 and 2000). I should like to thank Jan von Holleben and my wife Jessica for help with some points of translation.